LAGRANGE COUNTY PUBLIC LIBRARY

3 0477 10126 0705

**j633.1
KNU**

**KNUTSON, JULIE
SEED TO STOVE**

OFFICIAL DISCARD
LaGrange County Public Library

SEED TO STOVE

NATURE'S MAKERS

JULIE KNUTSON

Published in the United States of America by Cherry Lake Publishing
Ann Arbor, Michigan
www.cherrylakepublishing.com

Content Advisors: Andrea Hazzard, owner, Hazzard Free Farm

Photo Credits: © Courtney Oertel, cover, 1, 17, 24, 28; © Stanley Fong/Shutterstock.com, 5; © Julie Knutson, 6; © critterbiz/Shutterstock.com, 9; © Jessie Crow Mermel, 10, 12, 20, 23; © Sean Locke Photography, 11; © Kaca Skokanova/Shutterstock.com, 14; © kristof lauwers/Shutterstock.com, 18; © Courtesy of Andrea Hazzard, 26

Copyright ©2019 by Cherry Lake Publishing
All rights reserved. No part of this book may be reproduced or utilized in any form or by any means without written permission from the publisher.

Library of Congress Cataloging-in-Publication Data
Names: Knutson, Julie, author. | Knutson, Julie. Nature's makers.
Title: Seed to stove / by Julie Knutson.
Description: Ann Arbor : Cherry Lake Publishing, 2019. | Series: Nature's makers | Includes bibliographical references and index.
Identifiers: LCCN 2018036611| ISBN 9781534142985 (hardcover) | ISBN 9781534140745 (pdf) | ISBN 9781534139541 (pbk.) | ISBN 9781534141940 (hosted ebook)
Subjects: LCSH: Grain—Juvenile literature. | Farms, Small—Juvenile literature.
Classification: LCC SB189 .K58 2019 | DDC 633.1—dc23
LC record available at https://lccn.loc.gov/2018036611

Cherry Lake Publishing would like to acknowledge the work of The Partnership for 21st Century Learning. Please visit www.p21.org for more information.

Printed in the United States of America
Corporate Graphics

ABOUT THE AUTHOR

Julie Knutson is a former teacher who writes from her home in northern Illinois. Researching these books involved sampling a range of farm products, from local honey to heirloom grains to…farm fresh ice cream! She's thankful to all those who accompanied her on these culinary excursions—most notably to the young ones: Theo, Will, Alex, Ruby, and Olivia.

TABLE OF CONTENTS

CHAPTER 1
The Path from Seed to Stove **4**

CHAPTER 2
The Road to Farming **8**

CHAPTER 3
What It Takes **16**

CHAPTER 4
Getting to Market **22**

TAKING INFORMED ACTION 30
GLOSSARY 31
FURTHER READING 32
INDEX 32

CHAPTER 1

The Path from Seed to Stove

It's dinnertime! What's on the menu? Bread? Fruit? Vegetables? Cheese? Meat?

Or is it some combination of the above (like pineapple and ham pizza!)?

While we're asking questions, let's add a few more: Who grew or made what you are eating? Where was it grown? How did it get to your table?

Some foods travel a very long way to get to your table. They may start as a seed in a far-off field and end up being harvested, processed, boxed, shipped, and shelved.

A Hawaiian pizza includes meat, dairy, vegetables, fruits, and grains!

It can take weeks for a head of broccoli, stalk of celery, or spear of asparagus to reach your grocery store's shelves.

Take a look at these supermarket fruits. How far do you think they've traveled? It turns out that even simple, unprocessed foods rack up thousands of miles and change many hands to get to your plate.

- Watermelon: 791 miles (1,273 kilometers)
- Apples: 1,555 miles (2,502 km)
- Peaches: 1,674 miles (2,694 km)
- Strawberries: 1,944 miles (3,128 km)
- Grapes: 2,142 miles (3,447 km)

Foods that require factory processing—some cheeses, breads, meats, and grains—take many more steps to get to your grocery store.

It all adds up to a lot of distance between producer and **consumer**, seed and stove.

Do all foods crisscross states, countries, and continents to get to your table? Are there always so many miles, steps, and people between you and your food?

The simple answer is no.

It's definitely not the case for Andrea (Andy) Hazzard. Andy is a farmer who lives in northern Illinois and grows **heirloom** grains. When Andy makes cornbread, oatmeal, or cakes, she uses resources planted, **cultivated,** and **milled** right on her farm.

Andy harnesses **human capital, physical capital,** and **natural resources** to bring delicious food not only to her table, but also to customers in her community.

CHAPTER 2

The Road to Farming

Andy's roots on this farm run deep: this was her childhood home. She grew up riding horses across its fields and making cider from its orchard's apples.

As a child, she watched seeds transform into plants, and plants transform into food. One of her favorite memories was working with her grandpa to make meal, or crushed grain, out of the farm's corn. Together, they picked corn from the old crib and shelled it, kernel by kernel. Then, they would use a hand-cranked grinder to make cornmeal. The

A corn crib is a place where corn is stored and dried.

Hazzard Free welcomes visitors to share in farm experiences through field days and farm dinners.

next stop was the kitchen, where Andy and her grandmother molded the meal into cakes and cooked them on the griddle.

For Andy, really *knowing* how her food was produced was a magical part of childhood. She didn't realize its importance then, but it would be a major factor in her decision to become a farmer.

Learning to cook with her grandmother was an important moment for Andy.
What has your family taught you?

11

Today, Andy shares her knowledge with new farmers.

"That single thing changed the course of my life. The fact that he shared that very basic thing of how to take an ear of corn and make a corn cake out of it changed the course of my life."

—Andrea Hazzard

Later, as a young adult, Andy worked on a prairie restoration project. Prairie restoration reintroduces native plants and grasses to the landscape in order to prevent soil **erosion**.

The project made her think about how farming can affect the land. She developed a love for seeds, especially **ancient** and heirloom varieties. She learned how to go into fields, assess plant health, and hand-harvest the best seeds. She came to see seeds as a key piece of our human history. She also came to believe that plant diversity is needed to support soil and animal health.

Throughout all these experiences working with the land, Andy listened to and learned from the people around her. When it came time to start her own farm, she had a wealth of knowledge to apply.

Norway's Svalbard Global Seed Vault is the planet's main site for the safekeeping of seeds. The remote, Arctic site is located just 810 miles (1,304 km) from the North Pole.

Svalbard Global Seed Vault

According to the United Nations, less than 3 percent of the more than 250,000 plant varieties available for agriculture are currently used. Today, more than half of the world's "food energy" comes from three crops: corn (maize), rice, and wheat. Does this movement toward **monoculture** impact our environment? Is agricultural diversity important?

Crop diversity matters because it provides stability. If one crop fails because of weather or pests, other food sources are still available. Andy knows this from experience. In a typical season, she grows up to 12 different types of grains on her 20-acre (8-hectare) farm. This provides "insurance" if one crop doesn't do as well as predicted.

It's not just small farmers who are interested in **biodiversity**. Governments and nonprofits are currently partnering on major seed-saving efforts. Norway's remote Svalbard Global Seed Vault houses more than one million seed samples. These could be used to restore plant diversity if a major food crisis ever occurred.

CHAPTER 3

What It Takes

One natural resource that all farmers need is land. This is a huge barrier for a lot of young farmers and one that Andy didn't face.

Andy's access to family land allowed her to start a small organic vegetable-growing operation in 2007 called Hazzard Free Farm. In these early years, she worked within the model of **community supported agriculture** (CSA). She built up a loyal following of kale-loving subscribers who would get a weekly box of the fresh veggies.

Andy also worked closely with local restaurants to determine the demand for certain types of produce. She

Andy currently farms 20 acres (8 ha) of land. Her family's farm history stretches over 150 years—they began farming in northern Illinois in 1847.

Community gardens are popular all over the world.

partnered with chefs to find out what foods they wanted, and embraced the challenge of supplying it from her fields.

Throughout Andy's childhood and early adult years, she gained an understanding of soil and plants. As a new farmer, she was surrounded by others in her rural community who

Garden Farming

Andy was lucky: she wanted to farm, and she had access to land. But what are the options for would-be farmers who didn't grow up in farming families? How much land do you need to get started?

*With Earth's growing population and shrinking land supplies, many people see **garden farming** as the wave of the future. These can be small, individually farmed plots or shared community gardens. In Detroit, organizations like Keep Growing Detroit help city gardeners become food **entrepreneurs** who sell fruit, vegetables, flowers, and herbs at markets and to restaurants.*

Urban farm programs have positive effects across the community. They provide access to healthy and reasonably priced local food. They also create jobs, beautify cities, and increase property values.

[NATURE'S MAKERS]

Andy's farm equipment includes antique tractors and tillers.

had spent a lifetime in agriculture. Because Andy had this baseline of human capital, or knowledge, she could experiment with new growing techniques and practices.

Beyond land and knowledge, farmers also need physical resources. These include tractors, milling machines, and barns. As part of a family operation, Andy shares these resources with her father and brother. She also rents some machinery. Why not buy her own? Equipment can be a major expense. A combine harvester that is only used a few weeks a year can cost more than $300,000!

Because of these costs, sharing and renting are often the best options.

A World of Resources

Andy is an agricultural entrepreneur, which means she coordinates resources (or **inputs**) to make products (or **outputs**).

Natural Resources—Land and Animals: Natural resources are just what they sound like: materials that come directly from nature. These resources exist without human intervention. Some natural resources, like the sun and wind, are renewable. Others, like oil and coal, are **nonrenewable**. What natural resources does Andy's farm need to succeed?

Human Resources—Labor: Human resources are the "people" aspect of any operation. In Andy's case, it's the knowledge, skills, experience, and abilities that she needs to run her business. It also includes any help that she needs from other employees.

Physical Resources—Capital: Physical resources are the things you need to help operate a business, like machines, computers, and buildings. What physical resources does the farm need?

CHAPTER 4

Getting to Market

Andy loved vegetable farming during her first few seasons. She especially liked the challenge of learning about so many different crop families, from Brassicas (broccoli and cabbage) to Solanaceae (tomatoes). She had great customers and a talent for growing produce without chemicals.

But she never stopped thinking about her childhood wheat fields and the open prairie with its heirloom seeds. While still farming vegetables, she introduced a few acres of grains. Andy started adding not just corn, but also ground cornmeal to her CSA boxes and offerings to restaurant chefs. Her customers embraced it, and Hazzard Free Farm branched in a new direction.

While Andy started her career as a farmer growing vegetables, she had the experience and infrastructure to do what she really wanted—grow grains.

Pieces of heavy farm equipment, such as this tractor, are generally not made for people Andy's size.

Today, Andy grows several types of grains, including oats, barley, wheat, and seven varieties of corn. She is the sole owner of her business, and her seasonal to-do list has more than 90 items on it.

Aside from the demands of farming 20 acres (8 ha), what other challenges does she face?

Farming equipment itself poses some unique obstacles. These items are sized for taller and heavier users, not for people like Andy who stands just under 5 feet (152 centimeters) tall. While many farmers don't have to consider whether they can reach a lever or if their weight will meet the safety minimum for a vehicle, Andy does. This creates an extra layer of complication in her work. For years, she even used hand-operated equipment like an antique walk-behind rototiller to plow her fields because it was a better size for her.

Other obstacles are more universal. Weather—especially too much or too little rain—is a concern for all farmers. Climate change is another major issue. Global warming is shifting what crops can be grown where. The stress of hotter

Andy works hard to hand harvest her open-pollinated grains in order to ensure the success of future crops.

temperatures is making some plants more likely to be damaged by disease. Farmers and their seed stock need ways to respond.

Andy's experience as a **seedsmith** taught her how to grow strong, **resilient** grains without chemicals or fertilizers. How exactly does this work?

Andy closely monitors her crops and saves the best seeds to replant. She looks to see how fast the crops come in. She examines stems and stalks for thickness and strength. She studies the corn to see if the ears hang downward to dry properly and prevent mold.

By taking these seed selection steps, she naturally controls pests and designs food with excellent flavor. Andy's practices keep with tried-and-true methods used the world over to preserve the plants' best seeds.

For many farmers, their work ends after they harvest their grain. The harvested product gets sent to a **distributor** who processes, packages, and sells it.

Not so for Andy.

Andy mills her own grain.

Andy handles *every step* of production, from seed to shelf. She plants, cultivates, harvests, dries, cleans, and mills her grains. Then she packages and ships them to her customers. Andy counts many chefs and restaurants among her clients. She also sells to **wholesalers** and individual customers through her website. This means that Andy—unlike a lot of other farmers—avoids the **commodities market** and sets her own price for her products.

As Andy's farm has grown, so has her reputation as a sustainable food expert. She actively promotes **regenerative agriculture** and works to help young people learn how to build local food systems. For years, she's partnered with the Roots & Wings Network in Rockford, Illinois. Participants join this program around age 11, and spend time learning about everything from weeding and planting to how to build a mini chicken coop. The knowledge that participants gain gets applied in a youth-run CSA.

What are Andy's hopes? She hopes to see a world in which a career in farming is an option for more, not fewer, people. She also hopes more food can be grown locally and sustainably around the world.

Taking Informed Action

Healthy Soil, Healthy Food: How to Compost

Andy believes that seeds are only as strong as the dirt in which they grow and that good food comes from good soil.

Andy's favorite way to build healthy soil is by composting, which is a process of breaking down organic material. Adding compost to fields and gardens makes plants stronger and healthier without chemical fertilizers. Other benefits of composting include keeping moisture and nutrients in the soil. Composting also reduces the amount of waste that goes into landfills. How do you do it?

Here are some tips from the Texas A&M AgriLife Extension Service:

1) Find a location for your compost pile or bin. Look for an out-of-the-way spot that allows you to move easily around it. Also, make sure there's a hose or other water source nearby.
2) Gather your ingredients. The tiny creatures that break down plant matter need an even mix of brown (leaves and pine needles) and green materials (grass clippings, weeds, fruit and vegetable scraps). They also need air and water.
3) Layer your ingredients. Start with your brown matter. Place a 6-inch-thick (15 cm) pile on the ground or at the bottom of the bin.
4) Next, add 2 to 3 inches (5 to 8 cm) of green matter to the heap. Mix the layers ever so slightly as you add.
5) Shovel dirt on top of the pile. This will add the microorganisms that will help break down the organic materials.
6) Water the bin or pile to keep the compost moist.
7) You can turn the layers, but it's not necessary. The microorganisms will go to work, and start making healthy soil! It will take anywhere from 3 months to a year for the materials to break down into dirt. Your garden—and the insects beneath the ground—will thank you for the extra-nutritious addition by providing you with healthy flowers and hearty plants!

GLOSSARY

ancient (AYN-shuhnt) variety of food that has not been changed over the past several hundred years

biodiversity (bye-oh-duh-VUR-sih-tee) a variety of plant and animal life in an environment or ecosystem

consumer (kuhn-SOO-mur) person who buys a product

commodities market (kuh-MAH-dih-teez MAHR-kit) a place where buyers and sellers trade goods in bulk

community supported agriculture (kuh-MYOO-nih-tee suh-POR-tid AG-rih-kuhl-chur) a subscription food delivery service that allows consumers to buy food directly from local farmers

cultivated (KUHL-tih-vate-id) grew crops on land

distributor (dih-STRIB-yuh-tur) a middle person who supplies goods to stores and other businesses that sell to consumers

entrepreneurs (ahn-truh-pruh-NURZ) people who coordinate resources (natural resources, human capital, physical capital) to create a product and make a profit

erosion (ih-ROH-zhuhn) the wearing away of something by water or wind

garden farming (GAHR-duhn FAHRM-ing) small-scale production of fruits, vegetables, or flowers for profit

heirloom (AIR-loom) a type of seed that produces plants with most of the characteristics of the parent plant

human capital (HYOO-muhn KAP-ih-tuhl) a person's knowledge and experience, which they can use in operating a business

inputs (IN-puts) factors needed to make a product, such as natural resources, human capital, and physical capital

milled (MILD) ground or crushed

monoculture (MAH-noh-kuhl-chur) the cultivation of a single crop

natural resources (NACH-ur-uhl REE-sors-iz) materials like land and water that occur in nature that can be used for economic gain

nonrenewable (nahn-rih-NOO-uh-buhl) natural resources that can run out, such as oil and coal

outputs (OUT-puts) the amount of goods produced using various inputs in a given period of time

physical capital (FIZ-ih-kuhl KAP-ih-tuhl) resources like machines and equipment that people need to run a business

regenerative agriculture (ree-JEN-uh-ruh-tiv AG-rih-kuhl-chur) a farming practice that seeks to build soil and increase biodiversity

resilient (rih-ZIL-yunt) able to handle harsh conditions

seedsmith (SEED-smith) an expert in harvesting seeds

wholesalers (HOLE-sale-urz) people who sell goods in large quantities to retailers like grocery stores, who then sell the goods to consumers

FURTHER READING

Banyard, Antonia, and Paula Ayer. *Eat Up! An Infographic Exploration of Food.* Toronto: Annick Press, 2017.

Mason, Paul. *How Big Is Your Food Footprint?* New York: Marshall Cavendish Benchmark, 2009.

Mickelson, Trina. *Free-Range Farming.* Minneapolis: Lerner Publications, 2016.

Reeves, Diane Lindsey. *Food & Natural Resources: Exploring Career Pathways.* Ann Arbor, MI: Cherry Lake Publishing, 2017.

Vogel, Julia. *Save the Planet: Local Farms and Sustainable Foods.* Ann Arbor, MI: Cherry Lake Publishing, 2010.

INDEX

agricultural entrepreneurs, 21
agriculture, regenerative, 29

biodiversity, 15

capital, 7, 20, 21
community gardens, 18, 19
composting, 30
corn, 8, 9, 12, 15, 22, 25
CSA (community supported agriculture), 16, 22, 29

diversity, crop, 13, 15

equipment, farm, 20–21, 24, 25

farming
    getting products to market, 22–29
    how one farmer got started, 8–13

food
    energy, 15
    how far it travels, 6, 7

garden farming, 19
Global Seed Vault, 14, 15
grains, 7, 13, 15, 22, 23, 25, 26, 27

Hazzard, Andrea (Andy), 7, 8–13, 17, 22–29
Hazzard Free Farm, 10, 15
    challenges, 25, 27
    getting products to market, 22–29
    grains, 22, 23, 25, 26, 27
    how it started, 16–21
human resources, 7, 20, 21

labor, 21
land, 16, 21

monoculture, 15

natural resources, 7, 16, 21

physical resources, 7, 20–21

regenerative agriculture, 29
rice, 15
Roots & Wings Network, 29

seeds, 13
    healthy, 30
    safekeeping, 14, 15
    selecting, 27

urban farm programs, 19

weather, 25, 27
wheat, 15, 22, 25